Snap books™
Crafts

Room Decorating

Make Your Space Unique

by Deborah Hufford

Capstone press

Mankato, Minnesota

Snap Books are published by Capstone Press,
151 Good Counsel Drive, P.O. Box 669, Mankato, Minnesota 56002
www.capstonepress.com

Hufford, Deborah.
  Room decorating: make your space unique / by Deborah Hufford.
     p. cm. — (Snap books crafts)
  Includes index.
  ISBN 0-7368-4386-8 (hardcover)
  1. Handicraft for girls — Juvenile literature. 2. Girl's bedrooms — Juvenile literature.
  3. Children's rooms — Juvenile literature. 4. Interior decoration — Juvenile literature.
  I. Title. II. Series.
  TT171.H78 2006
  747.7'7'083--dc22   2005006898

Summary: A do-it-yourself crafts book for children and pre-teens on
room decorating.

Editors: Thea Feldman; Deb Berry/Bill SMITH STUDIO
Illustrators: Lisa Parett; Roxanne Daner, Marina Terletsky and Brock Waldron/Bill SMITH STUDIO
Designers: Roxanne Daner, Marina Terletsky, and Brock Waldron/Bill SMITH STUDIO
Photo Researcher: Iris Wong/Bill SMITH STUDIO

Photo Credits: Cover: (girl) Getty Images, (crafts) Tim Hicken; 4 (bg) Corel; (br) DigitalVision, (tl) Ingram Publishing;
5 (bl) PhotoDisc; 6 (bc) Richard Hutchings Photography, (bg) PhotoDisc, (tr) Corel; 7 (b) PhotoDisc, (bg) Corel;
8 PhotoDisc; 10 Mel Yates/Getty Images; 12-13 Tom Hicken; 15 Mel Yates/Getty Images; 17 Richard Hutchings Photography;
18, Tom Hicken, (inset) PhotoDisc; 19 (cl) Corel, (r) Getty Images; 20 (all) & 22 Tim Hicken; 23 (frame), Tim Hicken;
(inset) Getty Images; 24 (all) PhotoDisc; 25 (l) Richard Hutchings Photography, (br) PhotoDisc, (tr) Alamy Images;
26 Richard Hutchings Photography; 29 PhotoDisc; 32 Courtesy Deborah Hufford.

1 2 3 4 5 6 10 09 08 07 06 05

Table of Contents

INTRODUCTION A Room of Your Own 4

CHAPTER 1 Room for Improvement 6

CHAPTER 2 Color Your World 8

CHAPTER 3 A Shade above the Rest 10

CHAPTER 4 Sweet Dreams 14

CHAPTER 5 Living in a Material World 18

CHAPTER 6 You've Been Framed 22

CHAPTER 7 Wallflower Waterfall 24

Fast Facts 28

Glossary 30

Read More 31

Internet Sites 31

About the Author 32

Index 32

Go Metric!

It's easy to change measurements to metric! Just use this chart.

To change	into	multiply by
inches	centimeters	2.54
inches	millimeters	25.4
feet	meters	.305
yards	meters	.914
ounces (liquid)	milliliters	29.57
ounces (liquid)	liters	.029
cups (liquid)	liters	.237
pints	liters	.473
quarts	liters	.946
gallons	liters	3.78
ounces (dry)	grams	28.35
pounds	grams	453.59

A Room of Your Own

A makeover can make a boring bedroom exciting and old things fresh and new.

You like to decorate your bedroom with your own style, right? You need a cozy place to crash, listen to music, try on clothes, study, or just relax. Well, your room can have the special touches you want. It's not hard. Just add a few fun and colorful **decorations** and make over some of the old stuff. This book will show you how!

Safety First

This box shows you safety tips for making the projects in this book. You'll be using tools like scissors, hot-glue guns, and hammers. So always remember, safety first, and fun will follow!

Sitting Pretty

Drape a printed or solid sheet over an old chair and tuck the extra fabric underneath for a "shabby chic" look. You can also add brightly colored pillows.

CHAPTER 1

Room for Improvement

Little touches make big magic!

You don't have to change everything in your room for a makeover. Just change little parts of it. Here are some basic tips.

1 Paint your walls a new color that will brighten your room and make it more cheerful.

2 Make your room more colorful and lively with paper lanterns and decorated lampshades.

3 Are your walls bare? Framing one or two posters you like can change the whole look of your room.

4 Avoid a messy room! Keep photographs on a message board and little items on a shelf.

5 Cover things such as pillows, lampshades, wastebaskets, and pencil holders with brightly colored fabric.

A Dressy Dresser

Fresh paint can liven up old furniture, too. A different color (and new knobs) will give a tired old dresser a brand new look.

CHAPTER 2

Color Your World

Style starts with color!

So how do you figure out what your style is? Start by thinking of your favorite colors. More than anything, color decides the mood of your room. Choose a main color and one or two accent colors, then plan around them.

It helps to know what your "color type" is. Some studies show that certain types of people like certain colors. Do your favorite colors match the kind of person you are? The chart on the next page can help you choose your colors.

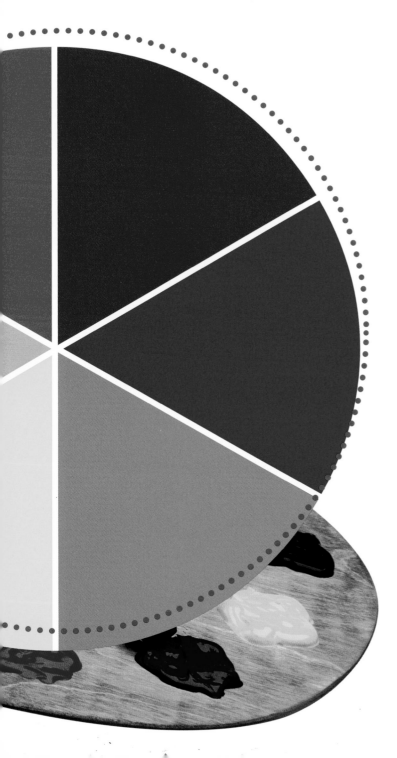

RED exciting, bold, lively, has a strong will

GREEN fair, calm, quiet, loves nature and adventure

BLUE calm, plans ahead, kind to others

YELLOW happy, works hard, looks on the bright side

LIGHT PINK sweet, happy, light-hearted, fun

PURPLE has dignity, loves life, has big dreams

BROWN content, steady, gets along well with others

ORANGE warmhearted, takes action, loves people

MAGENTA outgoing, has great style, loves fun

WHITE clean, sweet, likes neatness

BLACK bold, deep thinker, one-of-a-kind

CHAPTER 3

A Shade Above the Rest

Turn an old lampshade into a work of art!

Don't be in the dark about colorful lighting. Liven up a dull lampshade with color and detail by adding feathers, flowers, and fringe.

Your beautiful "new" lamp will brighten up your day even when it's not turned on.

Here's what you need

* lampshade, any size
* 1 yard beaded fringe
* hot-glue gun and glue sticks
* 1 yard-long feather or fur **boa**, color of your choice
* plastic or foam craft flowers (as many as you want to put on your lampshade)
* scissors

Here's what you do

1 Using hot-glue gun, apply a line of glue along inside bottom rim of shade.

2 Press beaded fringe over glue, starting at back seam of lampshade.

3 Trim fringe.

4 Use small dots of glue to attach the boa to the outside bottom of the shade. Be careful not to cover up beaded fringe.

5 Glue the flowers on the lampshade. Use as many, or as few, flowers as you want in any pattern you like.

New Life for an Old Lamp

Do you have an ugly old lampshade in the attic? Make it wonderful and fun with feathers. Cover the entire shade with one color or all different colors of feathers. Your decor will soar with this craft!

CHAPTER 4

Sweet Dreams

Want to feel like a princess? Hang this canopy over your bed, and you'll feel like you're in a castle!

Remember when you were little and dreamed of being a princess? Well, give yourself the "royal treatment."

You'll feel extra special sleeping under a canopy that you've made yourself.

Here's what you need

* stepladder
* yardstick
* pencil
* electric drill (for use by a grown-up only!)
* 2 screw **mollies**
* hammer
* 2 medium-sized metal **eyelet screws**
* 4 feet medium-gauge, clear plastic string
* scissors
* 3-foot-long, ¾-inch-thick wooden **dowel**
* 5 yards of netting or **organza** fabric

Here's what you do

1 Stand on a stepladder and place yardstick on ceiling where canopy will hang over bed.

2 Lightly mark dots on ceiling at each end of yardstick.

3 Have a grown-up drill one small hole at each dot.

4 Insert a molly and hammer it into ceiling.

5 Screw one eyelet screw into each molly as far as it will go.

6 Cut two 2-foot lengths of string.

7 Tie one string to each eyelet, knotting securely.

8 Tie end of one string very tightly around each end of dowel, knotting securely, and making sure dowel hangs level.

9 Arrange fabric over dowel.

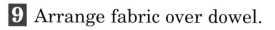

Safety First

Have a grown-up help you with this project by drilling the holes, screwing in the mollies and eyelets, and hanging the dowel for you. A stepladder should be used to reach the ceiling. Don't try this project alone!

Swell Swags

Pull your canopy back using pretty **swags** with **tiebacks**. Tiebacks are also used to hold back curtains. You can make them with ribbon, fabric, or strings of beads. Simply hang them from mollies and eyelets that are screwed into the wall.

CHAPTER 5

Living in a Material World

Fabric is one of the easiest ways to make your room more exciting.

Cover a message board in fabric you love, and hang your favorite pictures on it. Every time you look at it, you'll break out into a big smile!

Here's what you need

* 18-inch by 24-inch foam core, 3/16 inch thick
* 1 yard fabric of your choice
* 1 yard **quilt batting**
* dark marker
* scissors
* stapler
* decorating materials such as ribbons, beads, charms, sequins, or metallic wire
* stick-on picture hanger

Here's what you do

1. Place fabric on flat work surface facedown, then place batting on top.
2. Place the foam core on top of the batting. Then, using a dark marker, draw an outline of the foam core shape onto the batting.

3 Remove foam core and cut out batting and fabric together, 2 inches larger than the trace marks.

4 Staple batting and material to back of foam core starting at center on each side.

5 Pull fabric tight at each corner, fold back extra fabric, and staple to foam core back.

6 Decorate message board by running ribbon in any pattern across front. Staple on back.

7 Add other decorations that you like.

8 Hang board by putting a stick-on picture hanger on back.

A Shade Brighter!

Use the message board fabric to cover other things, like a lampshade. Lay 1 1/2 yards of fabric facedown on a work surface and roll the lampshade across the fabric, tracing the bottom and top edges with a dark marker. Cut the fabric 3/4 inch longer than the traced lines, and glue it to the shade with white craft glue. Fold top and bottom fabric edges under and glue to inside of shade.

CHAPTER 6

You've Been Framed

Show off a favorite photograph in a frame that sparkles!

Turn a boring old frame into a sparkling new one for your favorite photo.

Here's what you need

* plain picture frame, any size
* decorating materials, such as

* pearls
* beads
* metallic wire
* charms
* pebbles
* fancy buttons

* hot-glue gun
* sequins
* dried beans or seeds
* shells
* old costume jewelry

Here's what you do

1 Remove glass and backing from frame, and lay frame front side up on a flat work surface.

2 Arrange decorations on frame, then glue them in place. Be careful not to leave any bare areas.

Spray Paint Power!

Spray paint your decorated frame with a shiny gold or silver paint. It will look like an expensive gift frame!

SPRAY

REMEMBER!

Safety First

Have a grown-up help you use spray paints. Be sure to follow all directions on the paint can.

Wallflower Waterfall

Let your imagination "bloom" with this flowery headboard!

Hang flowers at the head of your bed, and you'll have a "flower bed" in your bedroom!

Now you can have a feeling of spring every day, no matter what the weather is outside!

Here's what you need

* pencil
* 4-foot white wooden **dowel**, ¾ inch thick
* yardstick
* 12 yards of ribbon
* scissors
* hot-glue gun
* 65 silk flowers
* two 1½ inch nails
* hammer

Here's what you do

1. Put 13 small pencil marks across dowel, spaced every 4 inches apart.

2. Cut seven lengths of ribbon, each 36 inches long.

3. Cut six lengths of ribbon, each 30 inches long.

4. Glue one end of a 36-inch ribbon to pencil mark at dowel end.

5. Continue gluing ribbons to pencil marks on dowel, switching lengths at each mark.

6 Glue flowers to ends of dowel.

7 Glue a flower to bottom of each ribbon.

8 Space remaining flowers any way you like on ribbons, using around five flowers per ribbon.

9 Hammer two small nails, angled up, into wall behind bed, at appropriate length to hold dowel and rest dowel on nails.

10 Make sure to hang your new headboard high enough that your pillows can't crush the flowers.

REMEMBER!

Safety First

Always have a grown-up help you when using a hammer and nails. Never do it by yourself!

Mirror, Mirror, On the Wall

Instead of flowers, use tiny mirrors glued onto the ribbons for your headboard. Then you can really "reflect" on your bed!

Fast Facts

Bedtime Stories

Would you believe there are special beds shaped like giant pumpkin carriages, rowboats, and racecars? It's true! They're made with kids in mind, so almost anything goes in this line of fantasy beds.

Messy at Massey

Massey University in New Zealand is doing a study of "messy teenage bedrooms." It turns out that kids all around the world have messy bedrooms!

Go Wild with Color!

Go to a paint store and you'll see entire walls of different color samples. Some of the wilder colors are named for kids and teens, like Pink Punch, Periwinkle Twinkle, Purple Rain, Electric Blue, Outrageous Orange, Very Berry, Mellow Yellow, and even Lizard Green!

Glossary

boa (BOH-uh) long scarf made of feathers, fur, or other fuzzy material

decorations (dek-uh-RAY-shuhnz) anything used to make something prettier, such as paint, flowers, feathers, or fabric

dowel (DOUH-uhl) long, slender wooden pole with flat ends

drape (DRAYP) to cover or hang fabric over something, such as a chair or bed

eyelet screw (EYE-let SKROO) metal screw with round metal loop at head

fabric (FAB-rik) cloth or material used to make clothing, curtains, swags, tie-backs, or furniture coverings

mollies (MOL-eez) screw casings (usually plastic) driven into a plaster wall to secure screw in wall

organza (or-GAN-zuh) sheer, stiff fabric

quilt batting (KWILT BAT-ing) puffy material used inside quilts to add thickness

swag (SWAG) fabric hung in a curve between two points

tie backs (TYE BAKS) pieces of fabric used to hold curtains back

Read More

Internet Sites

American Girl Library. *Room Crafts: Add Some Simple Style to Your Space.* Middleton, Wisconsin, American Girl, 2001.

American Girl Library. *Room for You: Find You Style and Make Your Room Say You!* Middleton, Wisconsin, American Girl, 2001.

The Editors of Creative Publishing International. *Bedrooms for Cool Kids.* Chanhassen, Minnesota: Creative Publishing International, 2002.

Montano, Mark, Carly Sommerstein, and Matthew Rodgers. *Super Suite: The Ultimate Bedroom Makeover Guide for Girls.* New York: Universe Publishing, 2002.

FactHound offers a safe, fun way to find Internet sites related to this book. All of the sites on FactHound have been researched by our staff.

Here's how

1. Visit *www.facthound.com*
2. Type in this special code **0736843868** for age-appropriate sites. Or enter a search word related to this book for a more general search.
3. Click on the **Fetch It** button. FactHound will fetch the best sites for you!

About the Author

Deborah Hufford is a former staff editor of *Country Home* magazine and *Country Handcrafts* magazine, which featured a crafting section called "Kid's Korner." She was also the crafts editor for *McMagazine,* a magazine for McDonald's Corporation. Most recently she was the associate publisher for the country's two leading crafts magazines in beading and miniatures, *Bead & Button* and *Dollhouse Miniatures,* as well as the associate publisher for a book division of craft titles.

Index

beads, 17, 20
boa, 12
buttons, 22

canopy, 14, 16, 17
charms, 20
color, 8, 9

dowel, 16, 26

electric drill, 16

fabric, 7, 17, 18, 20, 21
feathers, 10, 13
flowers, 10, 12, 24, 26, 27
foam core, 20, 21
fringe, 10, 12

headboard, 24, 27

lampshades, 6, 7, 10, 12,
    13, 21
lighting, 10

message board, 7, 18, 21
mirrors, 27
mollies, 16

netting, 16

organza, 16

paint, 6, 7, 23, 29
pearls, 22
pebbles, 22
picture frame, 22, 23
plastic flowers, 12
plastic string, 16

quilt batting, 20, 21

ribbons, 17, 20, 26

safety, 5, 13, 17, 23, 27
sequins, 20
screws, 16
shells, 22
stepladder, 16, 17
swags, 17

tiebacks, 17

yardstick, 16, 26